Conquering The Emotions Of A Man

Dominique Van Ingram Sr.

Dedication

I dedicate this book to my beautiful children Olivia and Dominique Jr.

Preface

What inspired me to write such a book, were the difficulties I have faced in my life. Overcoming obstacles of hurt and pain, has made me into the author that I am today. I have experienced the bad side of relationships as well as good relationships. I felt like I had what it takes to make a healthy relationship, so I decided to write this book based on my own philosophy and experience. It was a tough start but I was able to complete the process. Dedication and consistency has help me develop the mind frame to produce the "Conquering the emotions of a man". I thank those who have caused tremendous grief in my life, without them, I would have not been able to continue this new journey as an author. I would like to acknowledge my family and friends for believing in me and inspiring me to continue. I would also like to thank the people in the world, who are starting to believe in themselves. I thank the women and men who have escaped abusive relationships before it was too late. In addition, I would like to thank those who have been and who currently are incarcerated; for their strength and vision. I would like to thank the higher power for giving me the gift to write. In addition, I would like to thank my graphic designer, editor, publishing company and promotion team. Thank you so much sincerely.

Thank You

Dominique Van Ingram Sr

Introduction

Conquering the emotions of a man, explains how men really feel. It speaks directly to women, but some information, is attended for men as well. The focus point of this book is to, focus on the mind of both men and women through a channeling new concept. You will question yourself as well as understand why you exist. Most humans are yearning, to learn different concepts in life this book will help. The contents of this book will increase your power in knowledge of the opposite sex, and life in general. Some contents of this book have never been spoken upon before. So prepare your conscious mind to understand. and implement the strategies and concepts of this book.

Chapter I

One thing I believe is that most woman, do not understand that they may be the main key to conquering the true emotions of a man. I believe that once they soon begin to understand the male specie from a different perspective. They will realize that we all are equal. The only difference is males appear to be dominant and in control at times but, that is only an appearance, what lies beneath our inner soul, within, is never understood. Because we have a difficult, time explaining them. Becoming sensitive is not something we pride our self on. Sometimes we are very emotional while watching tear jerkers. Sometimes we have bad dreams that awake us throughout the night, and we sometime expect comfort by our companion, but we as men have a

0

hard time explaining what we need in order to feel completed. Emotions are the reason. Emotions play a huge part of our everyday life. Everything we do, the way we conduct ourselves is some form of emotion. Some men as well as women do not understand these emotions, which are very uncontrollable. I believe a man in general, is misguided by these unpredictable emotions. We tend to let emotions determine our core existence. We as men are prune by one emotion called the eagle emotion, which the eagle emotion is love, affection: Gentle courtship behavior such as mutual preening or sharing. This emotion is what we as men lack but we have no idea it exists. I believe, my philosophy is women are experts relating to this emotion. If women realize this emotion is considered vital. Then they may begin to understand what lies beneath the surface of the hard shell of a man. The conquering process takes time, just as much time as anything that is worth being, mastered. Mastering this emotion will help your companion, realize that it is, ok to tap into their inner self and not seem vulnerable or considerably weak. It is important to express to your mate that sensitivity is ok! Embracing sensitivity requires a lot of time as well as dedication depending on the person which embracing sensitivity is focus. The world alone makes it very difficult to become emotionally stable reason being, everyday challenges that we face, especially the challenges we face as men. We are victims of society, as well as victims of our own DNA. Images as well as currency, creates a world for men and women that makes the human mind think that having enough is not enough. Imagine how it feels to be, considered less of, or unworthy. Imagine the thoughts perceived by a man that cannot provide for his family, thoughts of a man that cannot apply for great jobs or pursue a career because his background limits his advancement. Then you have those men who have excelled at these points in their life but their thought process is a little similar. The only difference is one-man thinks about having it all while the other thinks about losing it all. We men have many battles that we face daily; it is very hard to determine the battles we face, because of our outer shell. You would never know what exists in our hearts. However, within are emotions at an all-time high. Emotions that we cannot control as well as emotions that we never knew existed. We tend to react at the moment, but not realizing that severe consequences follow the choices we make. The human mind when you wake up in the morning, may perceive that the Sun is rising, hear a few birds singing, and maybe even feel happiness as the morning breeze crosses your face. In other words, you are conscious. Unconscious contains all sorts of significant and disturbing material, which we need to keep out of awareness because they are too threatening and complex to understand. Knowing that this exist, knows that there is a possibility to conquer the emotions of a man. You must pay attention and realize who you really are. Do you really know? Alternatively, do others determine who you are? When you look in the mirror, do you know the person you are looking at? Does the mirror know what it is looking at? When you look in the mirror you are looking at your unseen spirit, you are looking at what will, be seen when you depart this life. You must understand what you see. The only time you are able to correct flaws of yourself is by looking at reflections of yourself. What do people see when they look at you? What image are you portraying deep down do you know? Men must know who they are especially as a man. In addition, they must not let the world determine their existence. We must learn how to crack open this mystery, I believe women have the key. Women can make and break their companion, but at the same time help produce feelings their mate never knew existed. If the woman allows a man to express himself, if she creates a sense of caring. She can install this into the conscious mind of the man which whom she is engaged with. This will enable the man to become open to expressing how he really feels. The woman can help a man find his true self. If the woman focus on creating a din. A din is a religion, moral laws, and values of your inner being. You must figure out what really motivate your mate. What angers him as well as what matters the most to him? The type of power women possess is phenomenal. They are the receivers of the world and are the reason the world Is able to continue rotating on its axis reason I say this is because, When a man and woman become intimate to be exact intercourse. A man ejaculates and when this happen the man release life, that is why a man becomes weak and remains at a standstill position. The woman makes no sudden moves she only receives the life that has transferred in her birth canal. At this time, she becomes subject to the emotions of that, man which she has had intercourse. She must be careful to let the sperm die first before becoming involved with another male. Reason being is because his emotions are living inside of the woman. If she does decide to have intercourse, she will allow these emotions to mix. This may result in mood swings or varies emotions, which calls for an emotional turbulence. Not realizing that this does exist may lead the woman in the wrong direction, which she will become equal with her recent sexual partner emotions instead of her on. That is why it is very vital to remain engaged with one; therefore, you can learn the emotions of your mate. It goes for the male as well; he must limit himself from indulging in

many sexual partners: in order to learn his true

self, from female specie. If we as men stay

engaged with one woman then the emotions we

release in her doing intercourse. Can and may

teach us, thee emotions that we never knew

existed. Pay close attention. How do you feel

when your intimate? Do you understand the

power this has on human emotions? That power

only exists doing the time of intercourse. We as

human beings call it pleasure, but the universe

calls it sexual energy. Sexual energy is the primal

and creative energy of the universe. All things

that are alive come from sexual energy. In

animals as well as other life forms, sexual energy

expresses itself as sexual creativity. In humans,

sexual energy can be creative at any level

physical, emotional and spiritual. In any situation where we feel attraction, arousal, alertness, passion, interest, inspiration, excitement, creativity, enthusiasm in each of these situations, emotions of sexual energy are at work. Whenever we feel these states of awareness, we must put our attention on the energy that we are experiencing, nourishing it with our attention, experiencing it with joy and keeping it alive within. How is this possible? Well it is simple. Learn from your core existence your DNA. As well, as learn from your mate also. Sometimes we as men have a difficult time realizing what sexual attraction really is. We tend to look at a woman image. Such as her breast size, her waist size as well as her weight. The way her hair, nails, make-up appear to be so flawless. We seem to become driven, by the outer image. We are attracted to the physical image instead of learning who the woman really is mentally. When men look at women our first thought is, Wow I would love to (explicit) her. We do not look at a woman and say, I wonder if she and I can become something great or have children and pursue the American dream. Society has planted the image that we consider the way. To my understanding, it is not the way. We as men must be very careful on the images we view. Because we tend to dissect those images mentally and once dissected properly, they become a part of our everyday life. We tend to respond to situations that we believe to be the way without actually knowing the way. I believe this may be from experiencing the images that we previously dissected. Images pertaining to money, women, and cars we strive to obtain these things, which are never fully obtainable. We tend to believe we can never have enough. This is why it is very vital; to have a companion that understands this concept. Not having the right mate will limit your potential power. The type of power you have sometimes develops through heartache. Others may already possess this power not realizing it. Your mate plays a huge roll in strengthen your potential power. You must understand their flaws first. If you do not understand there flaws you will not be able to understand where the underlying problem exist. Many do not understand that many men as well as woman have wounds that have never had the time to begin a healing process. It may be from childhood, it may even be from a previous relationship. Whatever the case may be please, understand these wounds still exist underneath the outer shell. A person image may appear to be in a great physical working condition but their mind may be in a very susceptible state. That is why it is extremely important to realize who a person is mentally. You must understand the mind in order to understand your companion. This will be very difficult but will be able to be conquered. I believe many throw the towel in to soon by not realizing, that success is just around the corner. Giving in suddenly, may be the easy way. However, I encourage you to with stand the battle. You must understand doing this battle (like all battles) there will be a winner and a loser. Once you enter this battle prepare yourself mentally which will take proper preparation. This is a battle not physical, but spiritual. Once realized then the conquering of the mind process can begin. Prepare to be approached by forces that or unseen to the naked eye. There will be many thoughts that indicate no success. As well as thoughts that indicate, success is possible, at this time when you begin to hear these thoughts. You must learn how to discern the right thoughts from the wrong thoughts. In order to achieve this, your mind must understand what it is listening and seeing. Be careful not to answer to every thought formed, because this can cause difficulties in producing the right decision. Remember that the human mind has never been fully conquered. However, do not get discouraged. Anything worth mastering, will take patience and self-control understand mastering men emotions is a very difficult task but if done

properly the results are phenomenal. Some

women have an Idea of what drives a man while

others have no clue. Most men enjoy being the

center of attention as well as the first to dominate.

When we are not, in the spotlight, we feel

defeated by whatever has taken the spotlight at

that moment and this becomes a problem, which

we only know exist. How do women find out that

this problem exists? Watches the way he respond

to other dominate males or those of a higher

standing. Does he engage in conversations? On

the other hand, does he use the option to listen?

Does he stand still? Posture is very important it is

a practiced or cultivated arrangement of the body.

Does he remain silent? Realize that we all were,

given two ears and one mouth, reason being so

that we can listen more and speak less. The more you say the more a person becomes familiar with who you are as a person. The key is to force him to engage in conversations more than often. This will allow him to express his core existence and give you a chance to understand who he truly is as a person. Most men are not as comfortable with expressing their feelings as other men are. So the question is what type of man do you have? Do you really know? Alternatively, do you assume you know? Have you really studied him? Have you really taken the time to learn his flaws as well as his achievements? What is his favorite movie? Do you know? What is his favorite color? Do not be surprise but some men love the color pink but society tells us that it is not ok: unless affiliated with homosexuality, which I have nothing against at all! Most women I believe think they have the answers to these simple questions. Nevertheless, in reality, the questions remain unanswered. Look into your inner self-first; understand your value because you must understand your values, before you can understand anyone else's. Value and self-worth is very important, it helps you determine who your really are, and the reason for your existence. A kind word spoken to an individual will effect that persons day. That is why it is very vital to speak positive. Speaking negative can and will have the same effect. This is why it is important to plant a positive seed in your mate. The more you encourage them, the more that seed will grow and begin to blossom into something great! You must force the greatness that is unseen, deeply in your companion. Focus on implementing thoughts of greatness such as, you are a wonderful person, I love to be in your presence, you can be anything you want to be. When you speak these things into the mind of your companion, their conscious mind starts to believe that they are and can become those things you speak. They begin to understand that they are valued! Once they begin to understand this concept, they begin to focus on becoming a better person instantly. Try very hard to eliminate the past, only focus on the present. The past no longer exist. I believe that many relationships end in turmoil because of past events, which have taking place. It is very critical to avoid conversations of the past. The only thing that exists is what is taking place in your life at that current time. Men have emotions that are uncontrollable but most think this only exist in the women atmosphere, which is wrong! We tend to hide them very well, our mind and heart sometimes does not align with each other. We think they do, but they do not most of the time. We feel one way but react differently. We want to show affection but most do not know how. Most men was not taught to be affectionate but was taught to be aggressive. If the woman shows aggressive affection towards her mate, it may scare him and possibly force him to abandon the relationship. He needs molding to become an affectionate person. This is not an easy task but may be accomplished, it you are willing to invest unconditional time into your relationship. All men are worth it! Why I say this, is because for every man there is a woman that fits him perfectly. You must be willing to invest, this is very critical. If you invest 10% then you will receive 10 % as well as if you invest 50% you get 50% do you see where I am going with this. You receive what you invest! So invest 100%! Moreover, the results will be phenomenal! One important thing that I recommend, do not force change upon your companion! This will only create a rebellious person. Instead change with them, that way they will not recognize your intentions and motives .Have you ever wondered why most men express the feelings they do? Have you ever paid attention to the way we react in certain situations? We tend to go overboard. We always will not to feel right, superior and dominate. If that is up for a challenge, we debate it. However, most of the time debating is not an option. We must be right, and we will not accept no by any means. Women must understand their true position why I say this is because society over the years has changed the true value of a woman. A woman worth is not valued the way it should be by society, it has diminished over the course of the years. We as men normally view woman as eye candy. We only view her through the outer shell instead of the inner shell, which will always lead to heartbreak. We always want what looks appealing to others instead of what looks appealing to the individual implementing this concept. We as men tend to want a woman who looks flawless. While not realizing that flawless will and never will exist, instead of getting to know a woman less attractive. Men want a woman that society will accept. Why, because we believe society will accept us at our current position whether it is at a great point of our life because we do not like situations, where we cannot provide. When we encounter this situation, it leads a man to act in ways he normally would not react. However, being the head of his household the woman leaves him no choice but to respond in ways that only he knows will benefit the situation. Which may lead to selling drugs or robbing? On the other hand, getting a job, this consists of 12-hour shifts 7 days a week. Which leave no quality time for a relationship or personal growth? Therefore, women must encourage their mate to focus on other options for attaining wealth, besides options that will lead to incarceration if she does not implement this. Her mate will never know their value or self-worth. Therefore, it is important to instill this. Now days, most women are the head of their household. They tend to have the best careers and earn a higher income than their companion. They are the decision makers as well as the father figure. This leaves some men in the state of mind, of dependency. This can force a man to have thoughts of not being beneficial in his relationship, and can cause him to overact and think irrationally. Many women will not understand his sudden change of moods, why because these are thoughts we tend to disguise because we do not want to give our woman any source of physical or financial power. It makes men feel less of a man. Not all men fall in this category but statistics says otherwise! The key is to create a dependency of each other! I say this because it can create an emotional balance beam in your relationship. If your companion believes that they are an important factor of the relationship you can help control the negative thoughts that form when they feel less important. Encourage your mate in everything they do, as long as it is positive. Do not entertain negative thinking, which will produce negative results, which will lead your relationship down the road of turmoil. If you implement this gradually throughout your relationship your relationship will gradually increase. Understand that nothing happens instantly, patience is very important and must be practiced daily in order for results to exist. Did you know that most relationships lack intimate conversations? Have you noticed? Most men are comfortable as well as women with talking to others about their problems then their

actual mate. The key is to eliminate this.

Eliminating this will produce great results. When

you engage in conversations about your mate to

others, that leaves opinions from the view of

others, which are more than likely inaccurate.

They only view your mate from the view you

have described.

Chapter 2

Men in most cases have a hard time expressing their feelings. We are very emotional but do not know how to use the right words to explain it. We expect our companion to understand how we feel, but do not show them how. We expect more from a relationship then most realize. We also expect our companion to know what we are thinking at any giving time. It is very hard to understand this concept but I will explain it. Some men think that women are beneath them and in that case, they are very wrong! They seem to take on the role of leadership without inviting their companion's opinion. We tend to do things on our on and what we say go. This is wrong! In order to build a strong bond relationship, the woman and man must be on the same page. If this does not exist then one will become more superior then the other. This will cause turmoil in the relationship. Some women (not all) understand the role of leadership and since they understand this concept, they are able to produce tremendous results in their relationship. That is why you see women married and you see some women searching for a husband. A man hates to be disrespected by anyone especially the one who he confides in. I know from experience that when you do not cause physical harm to your companion and they know you will never hurt them in any way. They become more aggressive, they tend to say words that will hurt your feelings as a man and challenge your manhood. They tend to disrespect you more often and when this occurs, the man begins to retreat. He will not say anything and will even continue doing the things that you ask of him. Lodged in the back of his mind is a way out. Any man that has self- respect for his self will not stay in an abusive relationship. If he does, then his self-esteem has deteriorated over the years. So when he finds a woman that is interested in him he falls in love quickly, without becoming familiar with that woman. He becomes someone that he is not; he is a puppet that led by invisible strings. He once was a No man now he becomes a Yes man. He begins to lose his self his identity diminishes. He no longer knows the reason why he exists. Moreover, trying to figure it out is too much work so he remains in a position, which he has learned how to become comfortable. When this happens, the man is not himself so acts of violence may become his only way out. He may be harboring these intense emotions inside, but talking about them only rages him furthermore. It is very important not to create this type of man. A man that loses himself is very hard on himself therefore; his values of life are different from yours. You must pay attention to the type of companion you attract. Watch the way he treat the women of his family and that will determine what way you should expect to be treated. Be very cautious and precise in decision making, reason why, looks as well as actions can be deceiving. Most people are amazed by the way; things appear, while not understanding that the image will soon fade. I say that to say this, a person may not be the best looking or have the best body, which will soon fade. However, what will not fade is the true beauty of that person's heart. Inside of a person's heart lies the true person, the core, the life the ambition, the hurts, the pain, and the difficulties of life. How would you know? You really would not because most people have a difficult time expressing their actual feelings. In this case, you must understand what is causing your companions rebellious ways! You must learn if their rebellious or if they are rebellious acts of his or her core existence. Sometime they may become rebellious acts because, most human beings, do not understand, how to activate their core existence. Once you realize what the core existence is. Then you will learn how to correspond with your companion in a way that you never knew existed. If you truly love your mate, and I mean really love them then learning what their purpose is in life will help you

determine yours. Do you think alike? It is not

good to have a companion that think similar to

you. Why I say this, is because if you both think

alike then you both will produce the same results

that I call, the CRASH EFFECT! In order to

become over achiever is you must think your own

way. You must learn your mind, which is not

your brain. Your mind enables you to become

aware of the world experiences, enable you to

think and feel. Far as you brain this is one the

most complex organ in the human body. You see

it is a major difference between the two. It is very

vital to learn how to distinguish the difference

between the two. If you think one way and your

companion thinks another, then this leaves room

for a disagreement that always ends with an

understanding. Have you ever paid attention to the arguments that most couples have? Normally it is a small problem, which leads to a major problem. I call this the gateway to (relationship turmoil) l. If you leave the problem small and realize that, its minor then your conscious mind will understand the concept and produce a positive outcome. If you proceed to let the problem grow into a major problem, then this is where the subconscious mind begins to work, which the subconscious mind cannot distinguish what is right and what is wrong. We all use our subconscious mind more frequently than we do our conscious mind. I believe that this is why couples are afraid to give there all to their companion. We tend to let the negative thinking overpower our positive thinking process. We are

31

very pessimistic instead of optimistic in relationships, not just intimate ones but all relationships. We as humans expect the worst! In addition, guess what if you expect the worst then you will receive the worst its simple physics. If you release negative energy into your mate then your mate is going to produce negative results, which will lead into problems that you cannot solve. Therefore, my suggestion is to try to release as much positive energy into your mate so they can release positive results. You must implement the same concept in order for it to reach its full potential. How do I do this? It is simple it begins with your thought process. The way you view things and the perspective you perceive them in. In order to change any circumstance you must change your mind, remind you, your brain has no dealings when it comes to your thought process. You, and only you, control your thoughts, that is why, it is vital to eliminate anything that is unhealthy and damaging to your mind, and your thoughts. If you do not eliminate the process of wrongful thinking, then this habit will start to manifest into your relationship. Once this happens then you have forced the universe to intercede. Which is also called the laws of the universe. Whatever you release into the atmosphere will surely find its way back to the source, which it originated. So only, focus on releasing positivity, that way when it returns after channeling itself through the universe it will return with a tremendous positive effect. It is your job as a companion to help build your mate even if it takes tearing them down, do so! Therefore, you can assist in rebuilding a new person, which

will result in a brand new creature, which will fit

your personality and dynamics of your DNA

existence. Does this seem hard? I know it does,

but everything I am explaining have been done

before and will continue to produce results I am

just explaining it from a different view also

known as my own philosophy and perspective.

Understand that using the universe in a spiritual

form will enhance your ability and increase your

awareness, not just in a relationship but overall

life obstacles period. You must learn how to be

aware of your mate's awareness even when they

are not aware of it themselves. Sometimes a

person needs that extra push in the right direction.

They may think they are on the right road but in

reality, the road they chose to follow is in a

circular motion. This continues down a road to nowhere. Be careful not to speak less of your mate to anyone. Never talk down upon your companion. Always uplift them and encourage them to be a better person than before. The key is to evolve, always become better then you were the day before. You do not understand the impact you have on your companion your companion trust you. They believe in you. They believe that you will always be there. Most people that are in relationships, never have thoughts of the relationship ending, this never crosses their mind. Therefore, when it does happen people are unprepared. Imagine the military going to war, without proper preparation, the results will end in disaster. It happens that same way when relationship ends suddenly. Disastrous, you never know what you can withstand until you are

experiencing with the problem. The human mind

and body is amazing especially when challenged.

Now these challenges can be negative or positive.

In this situation were talking about the negative

aspect. If a man constantly greeted by his

companion negatively, then he will respond in a

negative manner. He will begin to feel

unappreciative as well as the feeling of being un-

wanted. Which is a terrible way to feel? When a

man goes into the outside world, which is any

place outside of his home. He faces challenges,

which always kept secret to that man that faces

them. You never know what has occurred from

the time he departed the home until the time he

returns. He may experience confrontations and

decides to back down. Would he tell his

companion that? No! Because he is afraid of what his mate may think of him. He may have lost his job but is too afraid to tell his companion because, of what you may say. He dreads hearing those words you cannot keep a job. The bills due, the fridge went out or even the car broke down. When we hear these words, it challenges us as a man we become over thinkers and at those words, same time aggressive because everything falls upon that man! For an example when you were a child, everything was easy. You did not have to worry about food, clothes, or shelter everything was simple and at the end of the year you are rewarded at Christmas time. Nevertheless, you never knew the challenges your parents faced, because they did not want you to feel like you were not worthy. This goes for men who face those challenges today. They do not want to tell you so you will not feel unworthy and escape the relationships. Most men (not all) but most men want the best for their companion and children they tend to experience jealousy when they see other men in a position higher then there's. Unbelievably we men get jealous when we see our companion watching television shows that show more successful men then they are. When we see the expensive clothes, and house on the lake. The five star restaurants and the million dollar weddings. It challenge's us as men. We begin to develop thoughts such as why is she watching this. I am better than he is why I cannot do those things. These are the thoughts we develop without you knowing. We begin to feel not good enough, because we see that these images excite you. Therefore, we begin to develop an attitude! We start thinking irrational and saying obscured things. We provoke an argument at that particular time. The reason we do this is to express our feelings in an aggressive way. When we are aggressive, we expect our women to submit, but when she does not, this aggression turns into anger. If this occurs, remain calm do not provoke your anger. If your anger is provoked then the situations can become very heated, emotional and dangerous. You must understand that men as well as woman have wounds that have never had the proper time to heal. These wounds are still open, there just covered beneath the flesh, wounds that the person carrying them, have no clue they exist. Something a person says, may lead a person to become very angry why? Because of the underlying wounds that exist. They can be from previous relationships, childhood memories, or even memories of the present. So when your companion is angry then pay attention to the words you use very carefully. You can easily defuse it or easily invoke it. Most men tend to calm down when their woman agrees with them for an example. I know your right, which is a great way to go, I understand you these are just a few to name. Even if you do not agree at this particular time then agree at that moment, later on when your mate is in a rational state of mind then mention they were wrong and that you did not agree with them. Make sure you address them in a low manner tone and make sure there in a comfortable setting possibly in the bathtub why I say this is because when a person is in a relaxing state of mind they tend to not overreact as well as retain the information presented to their conscious mind. Look into their eyes and determine if there pupils are diluted if they are, this mean you have their full attention and they are aware of what you are saying. When you begin to doing this, make sure that they are fully sober .Why, because some substances can cause the eyes to dilute as well. At this point of time then you can ease other concerns that you may have because you have their undivided attention. So if you really want to open up as well. Begin to find your relaxing magnetism. Therefore, this time can become a form of compromising on so many levels. Not only will your mate get new information, you will also learn new things about yourself through the eyes of your mate. I have heard numerous times that men are emotionless and heartless. Years ago, I would have agreed until a recent study, men may very well be more emotional than their female companion. The only difference is men hide it better. In this study, conducted by neurologists at Mind lab, men are actually, much more sensitive than women are when it comes to being, presented with emotional stimuli. I believe that it is true. The good book backs these facts, which says that men were created first then women came afterwards. Therefore, in a different terminology women are descendants of men, however, women were created from men, so it is quite natural that they have less emotions of a man in some cases. That why I believe that women have the emotions we lack as men. Once we find our soul mate then those lost emotions will reunite in the most sensual way. It is very important to find who you are, meant to be with on this earth before your time expires. Therefore, you can understand who you truly are, once you reunite with your lost emotions then you will become complete. You will not be emotional completed unless this occurs. This is my opinion and philosophy. Do you know the true definition of a soul mate? A soul mate is a person with whom one has a feeling of deep or natural affinity, which is mention in the Wikipedia. Affinity is very important. It is only valued in close relationships and is a source of continuous intimacy. If one realizes that, this is an obtainable goal. Then reaching it will not seem so far away only inches

away.

Chapter 3

Have you ever asked the question what would happen to you in case of a tragic event possibly a death of your companion? These are questions, which most people are afraid to ask, let alone think. Life has many difficulties and it is impossible to predict. You never know what will happen at any giving time so it is always important to prepare yourself for the worst of the worst situations. In most households, usually the man is the sole provider and the woman is the stay at home parent. What will happen if the sole provider decides, to leave or pass form this earth? Where would that leave you financially? Are you prepared to take on these responsibilities? Once again, these are thoughts that we continually dismiss from our thought process. Unfortunately, this has happen to millions of people across the globe. Sudden disaster strikes, and when it does it leaves people at a stand still trying to figure out the solution to a problem they have never experienced before. Emotions exist that they never knew they had mostly emotions of sorrow emotions of pain and anger. Once these emotions arise, they are very hard to get under control depending on what caused the effect. You must always put yourself in position to be able to withstand any obstacle that may occur at any giving time in your life, such as losing your companion, at any giving time. We all know that life is hard at times and some people would just love to exit. However, why exit when there, is always a solution to any problem that exists in life. Pay attention to which you are if you pay attention to the small details you will never miss the big details. What is a small detail? It is anything that can lead to a bigger problem therefore if you pay attention to the small things first it will show you where the problem could have led. That way you will never miss the big detail. Notice that every moment spent should be cherished it does not matter whom it is cherished with. Everything that occurs was already predestined. Your family you did not pick. Your children you did not chose. Your environment you inherited. You did not have control over these events. What you do have control over is whom you decide to become your life partner. What you are is what you attract. If you expect to attract a doctor look at yourself are you one! Do you expect to attract a good man if you are not a good woman vice versa? We expect to receive what we are not. We want the sun when we are clouds that constantly block the rays. If you want to attract the best, you must be the best. In most cases people attract what they believe is there better half. Instead of attracting what they are. If a person does drugs and you do not do drugs, where will this lead? If a person is addicted to alcohol and you are not, where will this lead you nowhere! Therefore, attract what you are. If you believe in a higher power then find someone who agrees with you and your choices. Finding someone who does not agree will, only cause arguments and create tension in your relationship and life. So many people misunderstand this concept. Therefore, they have a terrible time finding true happiness. In order to find true happiness you must first learn how to be happy with whom you are. Happiness lies within your core existence, which I explained, in a previous chapter. Are you happy? Ask yourself are your happy with your life in this current stage of your life. Understand that everyone you attract displays a different form of happiness. Happiness to you may have a total different definition to someone else. If you learn that happiness starts with you, then you can begin to experience life from a different view similar to the first time a person who has trouble seeing first witness the beauty of eyeglasses and the effect it has on their vision. Do women look for happiness in men? I believe that they do, this is wrong, because it does not exist! Another human being does not have the power of changing your feelings only you do.

Therefore, understand the true meaning of happiness. A person may have the effect of causing false impressions of happiness buy buying expensive gifts and introducing an extravagant lifestyle. Nevertheless, what happens when that person can no longer provide that lifestyle? Happiness fades away! Therefore, it is not true happiness! Understand yourself first so others can recognize that you value yourself. Most important of all, is true value of self-anything that does not align with this concept is unacceptable from my point of view. Value is similar to respect, who will respect you if you do not respect yourself? Do you know the meaning of respect or do you have your own terminology. Some human beings believe one thing and it is very hard to change their thought process. If respect loses its value then it loses its true definition. This is not good at all. I believe men as well as women have a different outlook on this concept. If you respect who you, then you will respect, and value others. It will become second nature. It is a fact that some people believe there, respected in all reality they are not. Why, because, when you are treated a certain way, you grown accustomed to that treatment. You will never know, if you are respected unless you have an open mind to learning how you should be treated. A human mind is very gullible. It soaks up whatever it believes to be true. How do you know that your teacher is telling you the truth? How do you know right from wrong or is wrong right? Something to think about right, once a person tells you something always questions it.

Never accept that there telling the truth because, whom they learned their knowledge from could have been taught wrong as well. Therefore, it is very important to question all! Life- my definition is living in freedom every day! In other words understand your life is based on free will whatever you determine you want to become should prosper. Therefore chose a mate that follows this concept and nothing but greatness shall form. If you learn the concept of respect for yourself and others, your look on life will dramatically change. Continue to focus on your dynamics of your soul and spirit. People misunderstand, the difference, from a spirit, and soul, these two are different. A spirit, which is, describe in the dictionary as a nonphysical part of a person that is the seat of emotions and character. A soul in the dictionary is, described as spiritual or immaterial part of a human being or animal, regarded as immortal. You must understand the difference between the two in order to focus on each one individually. You may be battling with your soul while your mate is battling with their spirit. You see most battles are battles of self! When your spirit and soul are not aligning with each other, it forces your mind to contradict the truth. Your emotions and character must understand that this is a part of spirituality. Therefore you can focus on your immortal being side, which is always recognized as your soul battling with your spirit which is emotions and character, it is a battle that most people lose daily, the reason why is because they do not know that this battle is occurring. This could be occurring in your mate as well. You see sometimes, we think other people are the problem, but in all reality, we are the problem. We look for others to solve our problems for us. That is why we tend to choose the wrong mates. We see the problem we face in others and somehow it attracts us willing. Once again, you attract what you are! If you are living in poverty then quite natural you do not want to appear as if you are poor therefore you change you appearance on the outside to accommodate your actual reality. This is the same concept for others who live in poverty as well. You will attract poverty if you are indeed poverty! I say that to say this! Be yourself and you will gravitate those who a similar to you. Disregard secrets you have with yourself, these are wounds that you are carrying around and will not allow yourself to heal from, this is similar to the saying "everybody has skeletons in their closets". What you do not realize is, you continue to carry this unnecessary baggage around not realizing that it follows you from relationship to relationships including intimate ones as well as social relationships. In order to assist in helping others heal in emotional stages of their life, understand that you must heal you own wounds first. If this does not occur, you will become someone you are not! That is why most relationships do not last because we attract people on the accord of our wounds and once they begin to heal. Problems begin to arise. This is where the concept of growing apart emerged. When you begin to heal from pervious wounds your outlook becomes much more different than before. The person who you attracted when your wounds was in control of you, becomes to, look not so appealing anymore. You begin to resent them and say bashful words because those wounds need to escape from its source! That is why it is very vital to understand your true self before you emerge in the world with other channeling souls. It is best to search for a companion when you sprit, soul, and mind is at the correct balance point. When it is not at the correct balance point, your body is releasing unnecessary oxytocin, the antidote, to depressive feelings. When your sprit understands your soul then your soul begins to find the mind. Once your mind finds its focusing point, then your paradigm begins to shift. Understand that it begins with you first, in order to conquer anything that this world has to offer, you must learn how to conquer it from your point of view first. In order to learn anything you must dissect the contents piece by piece. Once you dissect the pieces you must put it in practice, not physical practice but mental practice is the key this will enable you to execute any plans you set in motion. I know you are probably wondering what does this has to do with conquering the emotions of a man this had to be, explained in order to get an understanding of the process. Once you understand what is happening inside of you then you will be able to understand what is happing around you. Take a look at your significant other what do you see? Do you see a person are do you see a person that has many things to offer? Unbelievably what you are looking at does not exist. You are looking at the shell of the soul. You are looking at what appears to be real. The body appears to be real. What is

real is the immortal soul underneath the image is

what needs the most attention of all. The soul is

what you must learn in order to conquer the

emotions. A person may become involved in a

serious accident. Alternatively, may lose a limb

or two or even suffer from third degree burns.

Does this mean the person's soul changes NO!

Only the image changes, that is why it is vital to

start with understanding the soul. Do you know

what a soul looks like? Studies have said, a soul

is made up of the spirit (intangible) and material

(tangible). The fabric represents us. It does not

have a location in the body, but is the entire body

plus our spiritual elements. Our soul is not

limited to our body, and it can depart from it. The

soul can be anywhere in the body. So if this is

true. Then there is no actual image of the soul. Therefore you can start anywhere on the human body. What I mean by this, is you can start understand the organs the most important one first, such as the heart. I believe this is where the soul is resting until awaking you will know if your soul is awaking by someone by the intense intuitive feeling, you experience. Some people call it love; I call it the soul waking up. You feel the pain the disappointments the failures and losses. The feeling of being rejected and not accepted is what you feel when your soul is awake. So in order to overcome this and conquer it you must experience it! Do you know if your mate is experiencing this? You can find out by paying attention to the small details such as describe in a previous chapter. Your companion may have been rejected there entire life, or always experienced disappointment's in one-way shape. As a child, they may have witness child abuse and neglect. Their parents may have shown favoritism to other siblings and this could of led to them feeling rejected. Their dreams may have been scattered, they may have had visions of becoming a star or achieving in an area that most people would be afraid. You see, you never know what your companion has experience over the course of their lifetime. When you meet someone new, you are trying to learn him or her in a short period. To determine if they are suitable to your wounds and pain which I mention earlier. Depending on the age of the person you are hoping to engage with, determines how much information that person has stored in there spirit, soul and mind. That is why it is always best to move in turtle speed when you are dealing with anyone new because your backgrounds are totally opposite despite what you may have in common. No one ever experience the same thing, even if you both witnessed it at the exact same time. I say this because everyone has a different perspective on ever situation faced. For an example, you may have only $300 in cash and the person next to you may have the exact same amount. You may be happy and make great plans on spending your money on things of your pleasure, while the other person with the same amount just lost their job and wondering how to survive on $300 for weeks or until they find another job. You see where I am going with this! Different perspectives are always best to view situations through your own perspectives. Your relationship is a product which you created therefore never console a third party (another person) because they will only tell you what they think is best for you, only through their own opinion not yours!

Chapter 4

Every man wants to be love unconditionally despite their flaws they may have. Every man comes from a different background but one thing that all men have in common are feelings! We cry, and pout when we do not receive things as well. We even call our mothers and cry to her, even after we are married with kids. We have emotions that need attention as well as women do. Why is it that, when a romantic time also known as Valentine's Day, the man is the enforcer? Why are we the ones to give roses, candy, and balloons? It would be very nice to receive a dozen of roses and a box of candy too! We like to feel special as well, like when the delivery person delivers you gifts in an awkward moment, such as a team meeting. You feel special don't you? All eyes are on you at that moment you are the center of attention. You begin to hear whispering and notice gestures, you recognize, but you pay no attention, all your focus is on the love and appreciation you feel at that current time. We as men love to feel this as well! We have no problem doing great things for women. Showering you with gifts and love is our specialty but, only when we feel appreciated and needed. We would love the same treatment, would you like your hair done? Would you enjoy a pedicure and a nice back massage? How about a car note paid? Better yet helping you raise children that are not biological there's? Well! We as men would love the exact same treatment! We love everything women do, how could not we

when we were carried and birth by a woman?

Unbelievably some men wish they had the

opportunity to carry and birth a child as strange as

it may sound it is true. Some men (not many)

men, think about how it would feel to form

another human being inside of their womb, I am

just being honest. This is a topic that is rarely

discussed, reason being, many people are afraid

of criticism! The point that I am trying to get

across is men experience similar, if not all

emotions as women. We express them in a way

that only other man will understand! That is not a

fact that is my own personal opinion. I believe

women are the source of helping a man reveals

his identity. Woman should open there heart to

anyone that is willing to open theirs to them. If a

man is comfortable with expressing his true self, then it is only fair that a woman do the same. If both persons agree on this term, then both can begin to start an everlasting relationship. It starts with recognizing that genders have the same emotions, some may be more intense than the other may, but they are similar feelings. A woman may show her feelings openheartedly while a man may conceal his true feelings. Most men understand why they have the feelings they do, but very few understand a positive way to express them. We have been, taught if we do not know something, then ask, I definitely agree! It absolutely works! If you are unsure about the way your significant other feels, then ask them! Never assume that you know what they are thinking, when you do assume, you assume the wrong answer every time. It is impossible to know what another human being is thinking unless you are, affiliated with a higher power (which I have nothing against) I myself is a believer. They say that the eyes, are the window to the soul do you believe that? I believe the eyes are the window to the universe of your existence. Your existence of your DNA make up! When a person looks in your eyes, they are witnessing a universe at hand. An amazing event that is free to attend. Many people do not understand the experience they witness every day, because some human beings do not understand what is happening when this occurs. This topic is, not discussed in our society currently. That is why it is very important to understand this concept. Sometimes when you are at home with the one you love dearly. Get out a notepad and take notes of each other with no limits on the questions asked. Do not be judgmental and insensitive to your mate questions or answers. Be understanding and receptive to what your companion is experiencing daily, this is very vital, it is very important to listen very closely and understand what you companion is feeling, if you listen with attentive ears; you will learn things that you never knew. You may even discover that you are not compatible, or you may discover the total opposite. Once again, it all depends on your perspective! A person must feel they can share their most intimate secrets without being exposed. The problem with this is that, when you tell someone whom you trust you are deepest secrets. They tend to tell someone who is close to them and so on! The cycles continues and before you know it your secret is no longer a secret, keep anything that is personal to you: to you! It is rare but some companions abuse this concept. Once you tell them what has bothered you and affected you over the years, once a argument is at hand then goes the moment when your past smacks you in the face. Once this happens, your trust becomes, violated to a point of no understanding. You begin to shelter you feelings, emotions that once were, guarded that once was abandon, has to return and protect its most prize possession YOU! Understand over the course of your life expectance that you will suffer major loses and disappointments that will shape your future. It could shape you for the best or worst it all depends on your predestined purpose. Learn to orchestrate your mate's thoughts in a way that is pleasing to their body, mind and soul.

Understand that most people are not subject to

mind control, which also known as mind games.

This is a major issue in many intimate

relationships. One person may feel that they have

less control over their companion. This is not

good at all because, you do not know the mental

condition of that person. One person may be able

to deal with insults and disrespect while another

person may not take it so lightly. You have to be

extremely, careful on the words, you chose to

address every person, and whom you come

involved. Once again, you never will be able to

read anyone's mind no matter how many books

you read or seminars you attend it will not

happen! Most women I believe try to read their

significant others mind. Why would you want to

do this, when you do not even know how to read your own mind? A mind is powerful and weak at the same time therefore trying to understand another person's mind will leave you not understanding your own mind. This causes confusion, which could lead to mental anguish when trying to figure something out, that you will never be able to do. Instead of trying to read a person mind first start with, understanding their mind. You do this, when they allow you to enter into their personal universe. A universe that many do not know exists. Have you noticed that you do not know you are asleep until you awake? Most people do not pay attention to this concept. You must understand your, mind chemistry and the way it works, in order to understand anyone else's. Most human beings understand what has been, taught to them traditional. How many people were, taught how to love? Do you really know? In all actuality, we do not. We only know what we have, been taught to that individual. Love is an emotion that is very hard to conquer, one day it is here and the next day it dissipates. How do you feel when a loved one passes away? Your heart is hurting. Do you really know what you are feeling? According to a 2009 study from the University of Arizona and the University of Maryland, activity in a brain region that regulates emotional reactions called the anterior cingulate cortex helps to explain how an emotional insult can trigger a biological cascade. During a particularly stressful experience, the anterior cingulate cortex may respond by increasing the activity of the vagus nerve—the nerve that starts in the brain stem and connects to the neck, chest and abdomen. When the vagus nerve is overstimulated, it can cause pain and nausea. Heartache is not the only way emotional and physical pain intersects in our brain. Recent studies show that even experiencing emotional pain on behalf of another person—that is, empathy—can influence our pain perception. In addition, this empathy effect is not restricted to humans. In 2006 a paper published in Science revealed that when a mouse observes its cage mate in agony, its sensitivity to physical pain increases. Moreover, when it comes into close contact with a friendly, unharmed mouse, its sensitivity to pain diminishes. Heartache has a different meaning to most people. I have heard that some men love, to see their companion hurting, it is true! Most people do not want to

believe it, but it is true. When a man sees his

companion hurting his heart becomes warm and

cold at the same time. He wants to comfort his

mate, but do not know how to do so. This is the

warm side. The cold side is the satisfaction he

receives, from seeing the hurt, depending on if he

caused it. I will explain. Many men want to feel

that their companion loves them, most of the time

reassurance may, be needed. Some will even go

to the extent of sleeping around, to prove a point.

They want to see the reaction of their companion.

They look for signs of hurt, or signs of anything

that is similar to hurt. When this reaction is not

exposed, it causes the man to try another tactic.

Such as sleeping with someone, that is close to

his or her mate, for an example a close relative or

close friend. Most of the time when this happen a man is trying to prove a point. His love is forcing itself to love in a different manner. A different manner that is hard to explain. In today society, faithfulness is not valued, as it ought to be. It does not carry its value as it did many years ago. I believe that some men (not all) still value this concept. The problem is that society teaches different ways of faithfulness. Society teaches ways to love that are false and inaccurate. Have you ever paid attention to what shows televised on television; it is a box, which sells other people's ideas. Ideas that are great, but ideas that are wrong, seem to be, advertised more frequently. The wrong ideas implement relationships currently. Ideas, that forces the mind, to focus on things that do not matter in relationships. Such as commercials that advertise expensive rings, cars, and vacations. Do not take this the wrong way: but when a person sees these images, it causes the mind to focus on ways to receive them, whether it is in a good way or bad way. When a person feels that, they do not have the means to purchase these things. It puts their mind in a depressing stage when this happens, the individual does not know it is occurring in their mind. This is when the subconscious mind is at its best. Most individuals do not understand the power that images have on their mind. Some do not realize that their mind is chasing these images in a way that is hard to explain. Some women yearn for the finest things that life can offer, but does not understand how much unnecessary power used, in a mind of a man in order to obtain her wishes. If a man is not able to provide for his companion, he begins to feel unworthy, as well as unproductive. Every man wish they can have more than they currently have, even those in a good financial stance in their life, form these thoughts as well. High successors such as doctors, lawyers, and successful businesspersons have similar thoughts. A doctor has thoughts of becoming the best doctor in their choice of field. Whether, it is the top cardiologist or top brain surgeon. Lawyers have thoughts of becoming the attorney of state as well as businesspersons have vision of making the fortune 500 list. Reason why, is the images that society plants on the human mind, once a seed plants in the mind it is, watered through images, which begin to grow. Once grown they become a thought once a thought is formed it is preceded by an idea which causes the mind to react in accordance with your pervious thought. It is very vital to understand the way your mind perceives images! What images excite you? How do you feel when your eyes connect to awesome scenery? Your eyes may never get, tired of seeing the same thing, same as your ears can hear numerous sounds at one time. The key is understand, what to listen for .I realized over the years that most couples end in divorce. Marriage is not sacred or valued the way it used to be. I believe couples end in divorce because the lack of intimacy as well as the lack of trust. Most individuals leave their marriage as well as relationships open, to accept others opinions which only hurt their marriage or relationships in the near future. If companions keep their most intimate secrets, secrets, then their trust window will close instead of remaining open, which will only cause constant conflict. Imagine life without a man, or life without a woman. How would the world be? Would it be the same? How would the world, be considered a world without the main characters? Have you ever wondered why it is only one man and one woman? Who told the world that a woman and man belong together have you ever asked that question? Men have a special place in the universe as well as the women. Men and the terminology of a man have a history that expands centuries ago. Before "man" meant a male, the word "wer" or "wæpmann" was commonly, used to refer to "male human". This word almost completely died, out around the 1200s, but

survives somewhat in words like "werewolf",
which literally means, "man wolf". Women at the
time were referred to as "wif" or "wīfmann",
meaning "female human. Part of the problem for
some men may be that they have silenced their
feelings for so long that they have not developed
resources for handling them when they do arise.
Such unplanned, unexpected emotions can often
prove overwhelming. The women have the key to
opening the unexpected and unpredictable
emotions of the man. She has the emotions that
men lack; she is the source and life of the man.
When a woman expresses her mind, it shows the
man the power and dominance that we love. This
then forces the man to follow suite. Reason we
follow suit of a woman, is because a man first
teacher is the one who has birth him his mother

(which is a woman) she is the one whom the man receives his first lessons. This is the most critical and vital time of the man's life. The lessons that are taught at this vital time predicts the outcome and shape the soon to be man's future. She is the key and start, of the undeveloped emotions of that child. In this case, I am referring to child as the man, not women. The emotions that are, taught at this beginning stage are the emotions of the child's mother. Whatever state of mind the mother is in at the time of birth is the expression that she leaves upon that child. This can mark the child, soon to be man emotional state. I believe that the emotions of a man can limit his true happiness, if he does not understand this concept. Women must understand the importance of their role in their companion's life. She is the reason the man continue to strive to become great. When a man feels secure, he is able to produce the best, which life has to offer. The feeling of security in a man's emotions is the most prize possession of a man. What I mean by that, Is when a man is at peace in his heart, mind and soul, the man begins to focus on how to better him, which will enable that man to make the best choices for him and his family. When a man mind is clear, he is at his best, at this moment, he begins to understand who he shall become, and the reason, he exists. Have you notice the way people physically look and interact, after years of incarceration? Their skin complexion and skin tone seems to be flawless without marks or blemishes. Their physical physique, seems to be in amazing tiptop shape, But most importantly their mind, mental state is in excellent condition as well. Reason being, when you're locked away from the world, and confined to a controlled environment you are limited to society, therefore you adapt to a world that doesn't exist to everyone else. You are limited to the images that destroy the average mind. When you are away from these images, your mind begins to delete life's previous images and restore healthier ones, which called the rehabilitation process. Once this happens, your mind begins to crave knowledge without limitations, it seeks knowledge that will only help the mind, body and soul and disregard useless knowledge that leads to nowhere. When you are limited to the outside world, you begin to see mistakes that you have made which lead you to your current position in life. You begin to notice your wrongs at this time, you begin to develop

strategies to correct your wrong decisions .You

notice a different person is emerging; this is

because your mind is no longer, polluted by, the

controlled substances and false images, you begin

to understand life from another perspective then

once before. A dietician approves the food you

consume so your body receives the correct

vitamins, minerals, and nutrient is which one

needs in order to attain a healthy mental state.

Your body returns to its original function zone.

Therefore, when being released from

incarceration or any controlled environment, you

are a new creature not physically but mentally.

This only applies to the individuals who reflect

on their flaws, and want a positive outcome. Once

again, this is my philosophy! You will never be

able to understand some emotions these individuals experience unless you experience them as well. This is just another form of how the emotions and body becomes conquered. That is why the woman is a valuable asset to the human man. She is in control of thee lost emotions of a man, if she believes that she is a valuable asset to the man then she can perform to start the conquering of the emotions of a man. Once a man finds love in his companion his trust is not disturb, some men ask questions that they should not ask. They ask questions about their companions past, which is a big mistake. Once they receive the answer they begin to express a not to concerned attitude, but really they begin to question the woman's past. Their mind begins to perceive images that has not and will not exist.

85

Some men even go to the extent of asking a woman how many sexual partners she has had in her lifetime. Once the woman is honest and tells the truth, then the man begins to feel resentful whether he expresses it or not. He begins to view the woman in another way then he should. In this case, the man has created his own misery, People sometimes create their own misery, in some cases, it can be, avoided and in others, it cannot. When a man asks a woman about her past, I believe that the woman should respond in a respectable matter, such as, I chose not to disclose my past personal life. If the man values himself first, then he will value your wishes and respect your choice. If the man continues to pursue an answer this is the type of man that needs to be abandon why? This man has not yet found his core existence, which I have explained in a previous chapter. If the woman pays close attention to her soon to be mate, she can discover many green flags as well as red flags. This goes for men as well. Green flags are what draw you to that person; they are the good qualities, such as personality, looks, and financial security, this is a small list so I am only stating the most common ones. Red flags are what you experience weeks are months into the new relationship, red flags such as outburst, drug habits, or mental and physical abuse. Depending on the laws of attraction, will determine which flag suits you the best.

Chapter 5

Many human beings live in pain and hurt.

Sometimes this pain and hurt leads to successful

ventures while others leads to disasters. Both

sexes experience these hurts as well as pains. We

tend to carry them around without dropping them

off, at the river in order to float away. The pains

and hurts continue to live within, the person

which whom the hurt belongs to. As a man this

leads, to irrational decisions that lead down the

road of destruction. That is why, it is very

important, to use your conscious mind, in

decision making, If not used in a positive way the

subconscious mind will overpower the positive

thoughts in the mind. That is when destruction of

the mind begins to form. Understand that no one will ever be able to understand your mind process reason being, your mind is your mind and you are in full control of it. The minute you begin to exercise your thoughts to others is the moment you lose control, because your thoughts and ideas becomes someone else's. I believe that you should discuss your darkest and deepest secrets with those you are intimate. In this case, I totally disagree because the one you trust today, you may not trust tomorrow. So ask yourself, do you really trust another human being, whom is capable of making the same mistakes as you do? A secret is no longer a secret once it is shared, the reason I say this is because, once you tell someone you trust, that person whom you trust, tells the person whom they trust and the cycle continues. Therefore, eliminate your secrets to other human beings even your mate. It happens every day in our society where couples divorce and separate, only to expose their former spouse or former companions deepest secrets! Now, I am not saying do not trust the one you confide in, just trust with limitations. Trust is very important in any relationship that you are involved in. Once trust becomes, violated then retrieving trust from that individual, can and will become very complicated. You may retrieve it, which is very slim. Alternatively, you may become lucky and regain a certain percentage of their trust back. Now the questions is would you accept their trust, it may come with ulterior motives. I believe when trust is no longer valuable it diminishes the relationship between the two individual's involved. That is why it should, never be violated! A woman must trust her mate and a man must trust his mate. However, what is the difference between, a real woman and a real man? Many people have their own definition, and having a different understanding, of this concept, only create imaginary boundaries. A real woman is a mature, sophisticated, classy, intellectual woman with strong morals & good manners. A real man has manners, is polite, and considerate. He is honest, open, and true to himself. He will fight for and defend the people that he loves. He is a hard-worker. He is not spiteful. He respects women and shows appreciation for all humankind. A real man is the provider of the family. He is strong, physically and mentally, and is never too proud to exhibit strong emotion.

Once committed, he is faithful to only her. He

does not watch porn or disrespect her in any other

way. He helps with housework and is a role

model for his children. A real man knows who he

is, what he wants, and is grateful for what he has

(which is stated in the urban dictionary). Most

people will not agree because they have formed

their own definition of what real might be. Many

human beings have a different outlook on the

term real! If you read the actual definition of real,

it does not align with most human thoughts. How

would you know if you are acceptable? What is

real? In addition, how can you determine who

else is real? Does society determine your

definition? Ask yourself, if you decide to follow

the urban definition of real, you may have a slight

different understanding on the term real. Many

individuals strive to become real, without knowing that they are already real. If you were not real, you would not exist. Society has changed the way people view this term, and as a result, many people have lost their lives to this irrational way of thinking. It is extremely important to understand and abide by the true definition of this term. So many people fail there self is because they are trying to win the approval of others. Learn to win the approval of yourself first, then others will strive to win your approval this sometimes come with a hefty price. You may lose those whom are close to you, due to the changes you make, and implement in your life. Nevertheless, you must understand that anyone who is supposed to be in your life does and will not cause confusion. If confusion is constantly in a relationship (does not matter which relationship it is) it will not succeed. In order to succeed in anything that is valuable to you. You must have people around that think similar to you, or inspire you to do greater. If your companion does not inspire you or encourage you to become greater then you may be in the wrong relationship or marriage. I say marriage because not everyone who becomes married, belongs together in a spiritual and universal way. Many human beings fall in love with image instead of what lies in a person heart, so it is true when it is said, what is on the outside, doesn't can't but, what is in the inside does. Many people follow their own feelings, which are extremely hard to distinguish from because feelings are a part of your emotional system and you cannot trust your emotions, let me explain. Have you heard you friend or relative expressing turmoil in their relationship? Have you heard them say I will never go back to her/she or this time it is over? In addition, in a few days you see them with that one who they have just bashed, again! This is emotional turbulence and this is why you should not trust your emotions. Only react based on facts, and what your eyes, have seen, not what your feelings, think they tell you. It is very hard to do so, but this is very vital, so do your best to try to change it. Now this process will take time but it is well worth it. Imagine how you will feel when you are not, controlled by your feelings. The results are phenomenal! To be able to break away from emotional chains can change your life in ways you would not believe. It is very upsetting that many individuals become, driven by there the emotions instead of their mind. When you are driven by your emotions, you tend to do things and say things that are not pleasant to you or others ears. Emotions forces you to make bad choices and react in ways you have never imagine. Most people let the emotion of anger get the best of the, there are millions of people who are dead and imprisoned because of this uncontrollable emotion. Anger is in a category of its own. Many try to conquer it but many fail. Understand that no one has the power to determine what you feel, not even your mate. You may think they have power over you, but realize the only power giving to someone is the power you allow them to have. Some believe that they can control others by saying things that are obscured and hurtful, and words have a major effect on people. However, understand it will only affect you if you allow it to. Sometimes a man or woman may say things, which may be very hurtful. Most of the time when people do this, it is wounds of their own that they are trying to heal, and they do not understand what and why they are saying these things. Sometimes the words they use are words others have said to them. Now this is not an excuse this, is just a different perspective on viewing your mate or anyone else whom you may be involved. Therefore, I believe anger is wounds that many disguise until, that wound is poke d. Now the question is what provokes and leads a person to anger. There are many reasons that relate to this difficult topic. Most problems become anger, which is, powered by the habit of blaming uncomfortable emotional states on others. The resentful or angry have conditioned themselves to pin the cause of their emotional states on someone else, thereby becoming powerless over self-regulation. Instead, they use the shot of adrenaline-driven energy and confidence that comes with resentment and anger, in the same way that many of us are, conditioned to make a cup of coffee first thing in the morning. This is an easy habit to form, since resentment and anger have amphetamine and analgesic effects—they provide an immediate surge of energy and numbing of pain. They increase confidence and a sense of power, which feel much better than the powerlessness and vulnerability of whatever insult or injury stimulated the conditioned response of blame. If you experience any

amphetamine, including anger or resentment, you

will soon crash from the surge of vigor and

confidence into self-doubt and diminished

energy. Moreover, that is just the physiological

response; it does not include the added depressive

effects of doing something while you are

resentful or angry that you are later ashamed of,

like hurting people you love. The law of blame is

that it eventually goes to the closest person. You

are resentful or angry partner is likely to blame

you for the problems of the relationship—if not

life in general—and, therefore, will not be highly

motivated to change (mentioned in the

psychology today source). So with this said,

many have resentful partners that are not ready

for change. It is very dangerous to try to force

change upon these type of individual. We men have a difficult time when our companion tries to force change. We become resentful and distance towards our mate. Our philosophy is do not try to change me you, knew how I was when you met me! This is a famous line. In all reality, change is good if it is not forced! Most human beings believe that they do not need to change; the only time they take this in consideration is when someone else brings it to their attention. Have you notice you do not know you have some sort of problem until someone else tells you: such as a doctor, a lawyer, or even your spouse. You do not recognize you have a problem until someone else does. When a woman shares her thoughts and opinion to her mate, it forces him to listen but react in a total opposite manner. Many men have a difficult time accepting their mate's opinion. In many cases it is up for debate, we as men do not like challenges by our mate but in all reality, it is good to accept this type of challenge. Anything that challenges our mind as human beings is a great asset to the mind. Therefore, a challenging woman is great only when the challenging is limited. Sometimes it can become overbearing and force a man to find other challenging women that suits his daily needs. When a woman nags, and expresses her feelings in a negative way it opens the doors for other women to walk into their current mate's life unannounced.

Understand that their will and always be someone that will be willing to do whatever it takes to earn someone that is worthy of earning. Therefore, it is important to keep the challenging of your mate in its limited source of comfort. Keep it in safe

mode at all times. This will eliminate many

problems and future turmoil and headaches.

Chapter 6

Do you know if your love your mate? Do you see the potential of a future wife or husband? These questions become, avoided when meeting someone new. Most humans express there greater qualities by concealing the wrong qualities. Learn the wrong qualities first. This may sound obscured too many but it is a great way to understand your future mate. Do not speak on things you dislike because, this will cause the other person to utilize your wishes and perform in ways you want them too. In other words, they will become who the person you tell them to become. When this occurs, you begin to learn a false and factious person. They conceal their identity and unbelievably many people are experts when it comes to this concept. Instead speak on things such as how far is the sun from the earth, or even ask a question that challenges a person mind such as why is the sky blue. Remember you are trying to determine if they will be a great potential mate, and it all starts with the mind. Many people choose the wrong mates once again because of images instead of facts. You receive what, you are, keep that in mind. A man will say anything and do amazing things to impress the opposite sex, so if you speak on what you do not like most men react on those words, and will use them against you but this is my philosophy. It is sad to say but some women fit into this category as well. We as human beings want what we cannot have, so if men believe that he cannot have the woman that he is attracted to

he will take drastic measures to acquire the

woman, which we seek to devour. That is why it

is important to understand men in a different

perspective then what society believes to be true.

So understand love first and what it is. Then

understand how to love yourself, you must fall in

love with yourself before you fall in love with

anyone else. If you do not learn how to love

yourself, how will you learn the love for someone

else? It is impossible to love without loving who

you are first. Many people misinterpret the word

love, and how it should feel. Never base your

relationship on what you think love is, know what

love of yourself is by far. What if we lived in a

world, without love, how would the world be?

Now days, it seems that love does not exist

anymore. Where is love? How do we find it again in our life and society again? If love were present, then there would not be many killings, or divorces or children growing up in single parent homes. Love has abandon many and the reason why is because, most people do not know how to love because love has not ever been taught to them. Many men as well as woman believe they know how to love their mate but they do not realize they only love, the way, which have been taught. If you learn your values and set morals for yourself, first then you will begin to recognize love within. When you motivate yourself and strive to greatness, you are doing this because of love for yourself. No one would love to see you succeed more than you do! Therefore, learn to love who you are in your physical body. The universe plays a major role when it comes to love and its existence. The universe forces love to return to its origin. Therefore, it exists when it is forced. When you are experiencing difficult times whether its misery that you have caused in your relationship or misery that others have caused you. It is difficult to focus on the right thoughts and feelings; sometimes you become so involved with dealing with others pain that you have forgotten the pain, which we normally abandon. Many strive for affection and sensitivity without knowing what is driving them to do so! We strive for things in life and in relationships without knowing the actual meaning of what we are striving. We tend to express how we truly feel to others then the main person that is, ourselves. How is it possible to explain how you truly feel to someone else? It somewhat impossible, I say this because, how do you know what you are feeling? Moreover, if you think you have a clear idea of what you are feeling, how are you able to describe it to others? Have you ever sat down with your mate and describe your true feelings, and once described, you feel like your mate is being insensitive to your feelings. Maybe because it is impossible to describe your feelings, you have to express them. Expressing your feelings is easier than describing them. If you are sad you cry, if you are happy you smile, when you are tired you sleep. Therefore, when you express your feelings to others use actions and understand that expressing how you truly feel will enhance the ability for others to understand your true feelings. Opening up your heart to everyone you become involved with is dangerous, and could lead to more heartbreak if you have experience heartbreak once before. Why return to someone who has broken your heart numerous times. This gives them unseen power that only they know they possess. They will always continue to break your heart it will never change no matter how optimistic you are about them. Some people use this to their advantage and continue to hurt others while not realizing that the universe will strike them suddenly in other words they will soon have a meeting with karma. It is their destiny! Human beings sometimes bring misery and turmoil upon themselves. If you do good to people it will natural follow you same goes to if you do bad to people bad will follow you. In many relationships, mates create problems that would have never existed if they had created them. I understand that over a period you grow apart and when this happen the slightest thing your mate do, such as drink the last bit of orange juice escalates to a major problem. This is because over the years or months you have had major arguments so there is no need for those arguments anymore; therefore, you start arguments over minor things that lead to major episodes. Not realizing that what you say and do effects your mate will leave you in a position of not understanding your mate. Realize that your mate may hurt you intentional in order to see if you care or just subsisting love! Many women, as well as men, do not comprehend the importance of pain, pain in an emotional way, not physical. Emotional pain is very hard to heal from, it is not as if you can go see your family doctor and tell him your feelings are hurt and he prescribes you medicine. You have to bear the pain that is present at that time it is very hard to endure. There will be nights were you would not get rest, nights were you will go to bed on an empty stomach, as well as nights that you will become sleepless. These are signs that states your emotions have become universally attach. There will be times when you mate disappoints you as well as time when your mate makes you feel like the greatest person in the world. Sometimes your companion and you family members may not see eye to eye, which may lead to disagreements. Nevertheless, remember you are not on anyone side, why I say this is because everyone that you become involved with displays different relationships. You and you mother, you and your

father, you and your siblings all have different

and unique relationships. As obscured as it may

sound, you may love one parent more than the

other, or love one sibling, more than the other, . It

is not right, but when the universe and nature

collide this may become ones destiny to have

these types of feelings. Understand that the

universe is there to help you, in order for it to

help you; you must learn how to utilize the

universe at its best. When utilize properly,

relationships will begin to change for the best.

Despite the way, you may think you feel, the

universe says otherwise. Most people do not

understand how important, it is to implement

strategies of the universe, it will help balance and

change the dynamics of your life and future

relationships. Most individuals are subjects of mate dependency, now mate dependency (which is my philosophy) is depending on your mate more then you depend on yourself. Many people fit the category, of mate dependency. Human beings tend to depend on others for love and support, without receiving love and support from themselves first. It all begins with you first! You have to understand how to support and love yourselves first before you can do unto others. Some individuals depend on their mate for finance support, which there is nothing wrong with receiving help from your mate. However, when you depend on them to orchestrate everything that assist your well-being, and lively hood this gives your mate power. Power, which many abuse once they realize they possess it. This causes a person to become more in charge than usual. Once in charge they develop in their mind that there mate needs them. Once this happens they believe that all wrongdoing is permissible. Arguments become more frequent, disrespect becomes a form of communication and physical abuse may become present as well. The key is to divide the power between the two mates in order to balance a prefect form of understanding and financial power. When both mates understand, the concept of equality they become better and stronger than before. Decisions become easier as well as life in general. What also happens is the process of emotions. Processing suppresses emotions, which involve anger, controlling thoughts, bitterness, and even unexplained feelings, may assist in accomplishing the outcome of a damage relationship. Many companions do not recognize that their relationship is severely damage; most live in a state of mind of denial, they tend to believe a lie instead of the actual reality that is present. When you hear the words I love you, do you understand the value that these words hold. Alternatively, do you not understand the value? When you constantly tell someone you love them the value goes down, they do not feel the way they once felt when they first heard these valuable words from you. This is a reality! Instead, say the words I love you, less and the value will increase. For an example, when Michael Jordan removes his sneakers off the shelves for a long period, the value increases therefore when he decides to sell them on the shelves once again, he is able to mark up the cost and receive a large profit. Because the value has increase, therefore understand the value and importance of using affecting words less in order to increase its value. Even though some relationships have suffered severe damage, there is always room for reconcilement if both parties agree. By not realizing that damage has occurred it will allow companions to increase further damage without realizing that it is occurring. This is very easy to do. Companions seem to blame others for problems that both mates have caused. Problems that may have been, avoided if both would have recognized the problem first hand. We as humans tend to conceal our problems and reverse them onto others, these is wrong. Understand that everyone makes mistakes the key is to learn from your mistakes and not let it become a failure. Failure is only when you decide to give up, therefore never give up on anything that is worth fighting. A wise man once said, "The day you begin to give up, is the day that success, is around the corner". Realize that every person that you interact with in your life will leave some form of impression on your soul; weather it's a good impression or a bad one. You must understand, why and the reason you meet people in your life. We all know of a person, well a total stranger that has influenced our lives for the best. We all have those vivid interactions that are hard to explain as well as understand. Think back to the first time you met your current lover, spouse, or significant other. At the time, you both were strangers, you did not know each other in any way, but you both made a huge impact on each other and this led to where you are now,

whether, it is married, dating or engaged. Think

about where you met your current companion,

and the location was it in a grocery store, a

nightclub, or it may have been in a park or

hospital, the reason I asked, is because everything

were already planned. It was your destiny to be

present at the same place at that particular time.

The places you met a stranger can, and may

determine the mindset, which that person is. Say

for an example, that you met your mate in a strip

club would this determine who this person may

be outside of their profession? How would your

mind perceive them? Most men do not look for a

wife in these places, but who can determine this.

Some individuals actually believe they can

change people's lives that have made a bad turn

in their lives. Understand you will never be able to change anyone, no matter how hard you pursue it, it will never happen, but what will happen is a person becoming irritated and when this happens it forces the person to do more of, what you are trying to change. If you tell a person stop drinking it is unhealthy, this will force them to continue to drink. If you constantly speak negative about someone else's unhealthy relationship, it will force them to stay in the relationship the cycle continues. When you tell a child not to play with fire, it is dangerous! The first chance that child gets to play with fire they will do so, no matter what the consequences may be. Some people, not all, believe they can change this concept, by not realizing they are assisting it. Maybe you met your companion in a nightclub, to many, this would say this individual loves to

party, or this person is outgoing and loves to have

fun. In fact, when you meet a person in a

nightclub you are witnessing a false image, this

image is not an everyday makeup of the person

which whom your attracted to. Nothing appears

to be real only what you perceive it to be. Do you

think you can find a great woman or great man in

the club or strip club? The answer is absolutely!

Many have across the world! Never try to change

a person based on the flaws and dislikes, just

announce them to the person and leave it all up to

them to make a change, when they begin to

change you will understand and feel that the

change is genuine. Couples strive to win the

approval of their mate, when this is wrong! You

already won their approval once they agreed to

spend time of their lives, with you! This causes the problems, which leads to damage relationships. Companions try to make their significant others happy, when they cannot, a person must become happy, with himself or herself first. If not happy within, then your ways of showing love to your companion may make you feel unnoticed or unappreciative. This leads to problems, which your mate may not know exists or may have caused. It is many people in the world that is happy, living in their own body; why not find these types of individuals. Life is like a blink of an eye, one minute their open, and then one their permanently shut. Therefore, never waste your valuable time on anyone who is not willing to carry the same milestone for you, as well. Many people put themselves in the wrong relationships; they are focus on the image of the individual whom they are pursuing. This is the wrong way to approach an everlasting relationship, seek what is inside the person heart and mind in order to determine the possibility of a great potential mate. By noticing, the body image first may lead to the emotion of enjoyment, which will soon lose its value. It is amazing the impact that a nice body and beautiful face has on the average mind. Do not be fooled! Looks will not last, but a soul will! Everything that appears, flawless is not flawless, whether it is a picture perfect relationship or a cake perfectly iced. There is some form, of flawlessness, that lies beneath the inner surface. Over the year, I have concluded that nothing is what it appears to be. When I see couples that are predominately happy all the time, what comes to my mind is what effect has come to past in order to present this image. Are they in love, are they under the influence of some sort of substance, or maybe they have inherited a large amount of money. What I have realized is people portray an image, which is not real; the image they portray is for others enjoyment. For an example, when you buy clothes do you buy them based on your own likings or others? Why spend thousands of dollars on items that will eventually lose its value. Over the years, I have spent large amounts of money on clothes and gym sneakers that added up to roughly twenty thousand dollars and over the years I have realized other options, I could have utilized my hard-earned money. I say that to say this, utilize the love your mate shows therefore the images that you portray to others is real, and

not false.

124

Chapter 7

Most men need the support and guidance of their significant other. It plays a major role on the development of the man's inner character. A man must be able to confide in the one, which whom he chooses. The woman role is extremely important; no one can produce the unfound comfort as of that, of a woman. Every woman is unique in her on individual way; this is what attracts certain men. The uniqueness of a particular woman can and may save the soul, mind and spirit of the man who is attracted to her. The reason many men achieve and excel at their highest points in life is the result of a woman; weather its, their mother, sister, grandmother, or companion. A woman has the effect on us men no matter what the relationship may be. Therefore, if this is true, which it is very well true? How do we men become great? It is simple to some, but may be hard to grasp to others. A man is born from a woman; therefore, his emotions are similar to those of the woman. Men sometimes do not understand these intense emotions, and we leave it to the woman who we confide in to explain them. Some women can explain them in most ways while other women, cannot. Reason I believe this is that women hold the key to conquering the true emotions of men. Some men have taking others life's and have giving their lives as well because of the emotions of a woman that seems to control men in a way that can never be describe. Have you notice, that women understand the way a man feels instantly, this is because he does not know how to express those feelings that has been harboring within. Some women take advantage of those feelings while others never recognize it. A man is the leader of his household only when he is the sole provider of his household. I believe that a man should provide for his family. Not providing is very unacceptable. If a man does not contribute to his family, then there is no reason for this man, to be treated, as a king. I know this may offend some men, but the truth is the truth, directly. At the same time this goes for women too, if a women expect to be treated as a queen or an equal partner then she must do her part as well, not doing her part in a relationship is unacceptable as well, to my form of knowledge. A woman may expect to be treated a certain way, such as royalty and I agree, but how do you know when a woman should be treated as royalty. When she is royalty

of her mind first, is when you can decide to

pursue her wishes. It is amazing how a man

becomes gullible from the present of a beautiful

woman or any woman. It is also amazing how a

woman can lead a man in a direction, which he

has never decided to follow. The thoughts, of

pursuing dead end paths eventually dissipate in

due time, only if the man is with the right woman.

It is very hard to decipher the intentions of both

men and women in relationships. A person that

may be interested in you may perceive the wrong

idea of you. Money is a major attraction; many

yearn to have it while others live without the

means of spending countless money on things

that do not hold any form of value. Although

money helps in assisting with making life easier,

it is not the replacement of true happiness. People strive to achieve large amounts of money, while not knowing exactly what to do once they receive it. It goes for relationships; many people enter a fascinating and reward able relationship, to lose it by there on mistakes. Mistakes made, are not recognize by the individual making them. If the man understand and appreciate the women, which he chooses to confide in, then the value of women will increase globally. Disrespectful and unappreciative women will remain at a standstill position in their lives if they remain in this state of mind. Most men if not all have a low tolerance or if any, when it comes to dealings of these type of women. When women disrespect a man, it challenges his manhood, and once a man's manhood is threating, he begins to develop the mind frame of no longer caring. Men no longer want to care for a woman who constantly, offend and degrade them. It leaves the man's heart in a gelid position, and once this happing is increasing warmth to the now frigid heart, becomes a tedious task to complete. In order to gain the trust of the man that was, or is still hurting from emotional pain, you must stop adding to the hurt. Some women, not all, fall right into this category. A man may tell his companion, how he truly feels, and soon as an argument happens, the woman uses his hurt and pain towards him. When this occurs it convinces the man that he can no longer trust the woman with his most intimate secrets. Although the woman and man may come to a mutual agreement, there will always be some sort of tension in the relationship from that day forward. A person is entitled to speaking their mind upon anything they choose to speak. However, understand that, speaking your mind my come with a high penalty. Sometimes the best thing to say is nothing at all. It is not always the best decision to voice your opinion weather you are right, or even if you are wrong. Many relationships fail due to wrongful communication, communication that is hurtful to the ears to dissect. Who likes to hear hurtful things about themselves, now I know constructive criticism is somewhat helpful, but I believe it should hold some sort of limitations. A person resent those who judge them, and in a relationship, judging can cause tremendous turmoil in the relationship. If a woman show appreciation towards her mate then her mate will recognize her intentions and grant every wish she ask for if it is in their means. Some women force a man to become someone he is not, you cannot force anyone to become something that their not willing to become. A man may feel under pressure when his companion demands the finest things in life, and he cannot grant her wishes. This forces the man to make wrong decisions and take actions that may affect the relationship in the end. When a man hear words of encouragement to achieve a woman's need it leaves him in a position that he no longer belongs a position where he no longer caters to his needs, but the women who he confides in needs. A man need to feel appreciated, loved and cherished by his mate. We men have emotions that need to attention as well. We are not always the bad person as some women portray us to be, we have flaws and dislikes like everyone else, but

we are human as well. Our love runs deeper than

the depth of the ocean for the woman we love.

We would love the same gratification and

apperception that we release and deserve. We

continue to learn the true meaning of becoming a

great man, some men do not understand this

concept and that is perfectly normal. Many men

depend on women, to help assist them on

becoming a man. However, what man would

share this type of information. When a man

believes in himself the world becomes a different

world he no longer see the world as other men do.

He believes in his dreams and will try very hard

to achieve them, if a man's dreams are scattered

by someone else it leaves room for

discouragement, which leads to failure, no one

should experience their dreams scattered by someone else. A man that believes in himself as well as his mate can produce tremendous results. Nothing becomes unachievable when both parties believe in each other; this becomes a bond that no one can break, a bond that is so strong that death is the only option that will terminate it. When a man believes in himself and his companion believes in him there are no boundaries that he cannot cross. Many couples place limits on their progressing stage as a couple. When a man focus on himself first, he can then focus on his family, but the key is for the man to be in a perfect mental state in order to achieve this outcome. This is where the woman's role is extremely important. This is when the man needs the moral support and guidance of his mate the most. The woman must assist her mate and understand that

this is very important to help her companion keep

a positive and creative state of mind. Doing so

will allow the man to care for his family properly,

without any discrepancies involved he will excel

to his highest potential in life. He will reach a

point that has never been obtainable in his mind.

Understand that trials and tribulations must exist

in order to redevelop your character, they are the

reason many human beings become much greater

then they previously have been. Catastrophic

events form and shape us as human beings as

well. This is why it is important to earn from your

current and past events in your life. I have had the

pleasure of speaking to, a much older woman

then I, she said something to me that would last a

lifetime in my mind, she said, "sweetheart life is

not always as bad as it may seem, remember there are people in graves that would love to trade you spaces". Over the years this particular beautiful woman has touch many lives before departing from her on. When things seem to go wrong in life, relationships, or anything that is troubling to your mind, body, and spirit, remember it is only for a short amount of time, never give up or in to any situation that may become to challenging to you to overcome. Relationships can become more powerful and fruitful if couples understand that problems never last forever. Problems only exist when the human mind perceives it as a problem. Most people worry about events that will never happen in other words, we tend to worry about things that will never exist. A woman may worry about her significant other committing sexual act as well as a man does. By not realizing that these are only theories and opinions and not facts, if leaves the mind to perceive inadequate information. Once the mind perceives these thoughts, the mind begins to perform actions. Now these actions may vary depend on what thoughts implemented into the existing problem. Thoughts such as your lover having sexual relations with someone else other than you can cause a major effect on the mind of the person whom has developed these thoughts. Understand that this will affect your mental and physical body. As much as we all hope for the perfect relationship, we all must understand no relationship has, and never will be perfect. Why I say this, is because most people strive for someone that does not exist. For an example relating to this cause, you never know what problems a relationship has. Some are experts at hiding these problems from the world. I believe when a woman constantly accuses her mate of cheating, that she is not doing so. However, over the years this theory was never, proven true. Maybe it is because the woman genuinely loves her companion and need reassurance of this fact. A woman has the same needs as men, men seem to expose their needs while woman remain discreet. When a man fine interest in a woman he does everything in is power to impress the woman in order to win her as a mate or sexual partner. Women on the other hand are much cleverer and more discreet. Women tend to keep their secrets to themselves for eternity. They will not let the cat at the hat. Men on the other hand will! When a man finally receives the woman of his dreams, we tend to show our significant other off to the world, we want everyone to see what we have accomplished. We want the world to see beauty, this is wrong! When this occurs, we fail as a man. When we start to accept the world's thoughts and opinion's about our significant other, these are when the problems form. We begin to acknowledge, the wrong thought and ideas of our mate. Therefore, we tend to react on everyone else's thoughts, but our own. We want what the world desires, and not what we desire. I have noticed that some people that we engage are emotions our feelings to, seem to have the biggest impact on the individual that is expressing their thoughts and feelings. They can say one thing about your mate and deter your thought process.

When your family loves and accepts your mate, it seems like life is at its most beautifulness 'point. When it is the total opposite, life seems pointless and unbearable at times. You may hear individual's say things that are unpleasant to your ears. This is only to discourage you. Realize that you are in charge of you, and only you, many may have different opinions. Nevertheless, we as parents are not even in charge of our children even though we think we are we are not, why? Because they have their own thoughts as well, that is why we must be careful what we teach our children. This is very important in all relationships as well. However, most people do not implement this strategy. Many couples believe that they can control their mate's thoughts. This is where problems occur. You cannot control the thoughts of other human beings. Why would you want to control someone else's thoughts? When you have a difficult time controlling your own complex thoughts: Look into your mind. Now let us go in depth. Have you ever paid close attention to your thoughts and perspectives of other people? Have you notice that you assume the wrong thoughts of that particular person. Nothing is what it appears. Looks are deceiving but thoughts are as well. Focus on your thoughts and understand them, then you will become familiar with the thought process of others. This will help you learn the mind of others once you begin to understand your mind fist. Most people fail in this category because they begin the process to sudden. This process takes time. You have to recondition your mind, over the years it has produce wrongful thinking in many ways. This affects different parts of your life over time. Many do not notice this because, they believe what they have been doing over the years is the right way to go. Now I am not saying their wrong, but I am saying many have been, programmed the wrong way. Because this has happen, too many individuals it has caused much heartache and turmoil in their life. A woman may believe she deserves the world, why another woman may believe she does not. As well, a man may believe he deserves the best things life has to offer, while another man believes he is not worthy. This happens quite often and it is due to wrongful thinking. Understand that you must be in control of yourself at all times. Never give anyone power over your mind, when you do. You become that person slave, which you are a slave to anything that controls you, or anyone in this case. It is not fair to the person, controlled mentally, because this says, that the person whom controlled is the weaker vessel: which you begin to become the subject of manipulation. Many people implement the art of manipulation without realizing it, if you tell your child to clean there room, and once the job is complete, their reward will be candy, you are using the art of manipulation. When you go to work each day and your boss assign you a job task, once the task is completed over numerous hours and days, you receive compensation for your work. This is manipulation. We use it ever day in our life and never recognize what we are doing. Having someone do anything for you and rewarding them is simply manipulation. Most couples are victims of this while not realizing, what their even doing. What do you expect to gain by gaining the mind power over another human being? This may be a question, that many people overlook, but few dare to ask. Using this against your mate will cause unseen problems. You never know the mental state of each human beings mind. Everyone you meet in your life has experienced some sort of mental or physical pain. By looking at a person, you will never be able to predict this. Some individuals, think they can understand what a person is feeling or going through. You may have a intuition, but sometimes your intuition can't be trusted. You may have an idea of what one is going through but, you will never fully understand how that person is feeling or their current mental state of mind. I say that to say this, your mate only express how they feel based on their current situation, therefore opening up and sharing their feelings is not their first priority.

Chapter 8

What do you expect to receive from your mate? Do you yearn for love and affection, or is financial security your motive. There are certain men that provide all of these assets as well as men who do not. The men that do not provide all of these assets that I mention earlier may have not been prune to providing for their mate. There may be numerous reasons why. They may have not been taught how in their life, or they may have been brainwashed by wrongful thinking. In today's society, I have met some people, who only think about their selves and no one else, these are the wrong type of people to interact with, because their best interest is not you but their own. Unfortunately, some men been taught that this is the way, not by choice but by involvement. Therefore, what do you expect from a man who only thinks of himself. In today's society many woman search for the right man, in all the wrong places, every man that has ever had the chance to walk this earth, has had great intentions of becoming a great man. However, events happen in a person's life that completely changes their lives forever. This can cause a person to react in a complete different way than you would expect them too. I believe that women should look more into themselves and find who they truly are before searching for a potential life partner. If a woman expects certain qualities of a man, she should also have the qualities she expects. This is where some women (not all) fail. Some women expect the most from there mate, but do not know how to express what they expect.

In order to receive greatness you must force

greatness. If you are a woman of great character

and high expectations, then you should search for

someone on the same accord. When a woman,

has a great job, or career, a nice home, a nice

vehicle, she becomes prey to less successful men

without realizing it. This is the same for men as

well. Individuals who seem to have their life in

order, attract less successful people, this is my

philosophy. When a man or woman engage with

someone, that is not on the same accord as his or

her are, one may begin to lose focus on

themselves and become victims of manipulation.

This is why it is very important to attract what

you are. If you expect a man to treat you with

respect and dignity, understand that you must

search within that man's heart to understand his hidden agenda if there is one. Learn how to utilize the universe, and it will always lead you in the right direction. The ways of the universe is never wrong! Try to speak to the universe and listen with attentive ears, it will speak. How you do this, I will explain. First, ask the universe anything that you would like to ask, once you have giving your request, stop and listen. If images, or words come to mind are your physical body is feeling awkward this mean no! If you experience excitement and joy, this means yes! Begin to implement the strategy you will be amazed on the answers you receive instantly. This may be a different approach for many believers of certain religions, but the universe is the form of life it is there to help and guide us, so utilize the universe as much as possible in order to activate your greatness in this world. It is ok! If you have trouble at first, be patient and understand that anything that is worth being mastered takes time, which I explained in a previous chapter. Life has many difficulties but your life can overcome the obstacles if you are willing to invest time into yourself. No one knows what the future may bring but we all can get a better understanding by knowing what path we choose to follow. I always told to follow your heart, but I realized that when I follow my heart it leads me into more anguish. Therefore, what I choose to do now is understand my mind from every perspective possible. This way I can understand if my heart is leading me in the right direction are misguiding into the wrong direction.

So follow your mind and the way the universe direct you. If you expect the best, be the best there is no other way to explain it. Never depend on just one of the three balance points, which are spirit, body and soul. If you utilize one without the other it will leave you emotionally unbalance and unable to produce tremendous results. Have you ever paid attention to your physical body when it is in a situation that causes tremendous mental power? You begin to unlock clues of your own mind that you never knew existed, this is the key to conquering any situation that you face. When you unlock clues of your own mind, you begin to discover your abilities that once where hidden. When you meet someone knew, try to assist them with unlocking clues of their own mind. People are born geniuses; some may have not learned how to find theirs. Everyone has a purpose in life; each individual has a special ability that no one else can produce but himself or herself. We all must learn how to value our true self-worth, unfortunately sometimes people miss the chance of a lifetime by becoming afraid of whom they may become. You have to take chances in life, when you take the extra step that is required to obtain your true self-worth you realize that you can achieve anything that you focus on. In an intimate relationship, much is required to maintain a healthy relationship. It will only prosper and bloom into greatness only if both are in tune with their three balance points, which I mention earlier, if not turmoil will become their destiny. Focus on your conscious mind and realize the power it possesses. Your subconscious mind will always interfere because

of its ability to believe everything it sees and

hears. This is why; you have to pay attention to

every detail that your eyes witness. Once you

learn how to use the thinking part of your mind,

which is the conscious mind, you begin to

understand things in a different way the world

becomes much easier and less stressful. You will

begin to see changes in your relationships. Life

will become glass, meaning you will see clearer.

Where you are in your life at this current moment

is based on the choices you previously made

weather they were good decisions or bad

decisions. If you made mistakes that have led you

into turmoil, this is ok; you only fail when you

stop trying. If you do not make mistakes, how

will you learn how to make the right one? You

must understand mistakes are a part of life and we all make them on a daily basis. The key is discovering why you made the mistake in the first place. Was it based on your own accord or someone else, is if it was your mistake that is ok, and if it was someone else's mistake that is ok as well. This is why it is ok, a person mimics what they see, and they try to become someone that their path will not allow them to become. Sometimes we focus on other individual's success before our own. We tend to believe what we see; this is when we become victims of our subconscious mind. We visualize the greatness instead of the upsets that the person had to experience before becoming whom they appear to be. This is what I prefer to when I say mistakes. If you learn the upsets and down points of anyone, you whom you are affiliated, you will begin to understand what to do or not to do this is when your conscious mind is at its best. It begins to understand pain and when it does it begins to process this information, once processed your mind becomes fully aware of situations that may become unpleasant to the mind and body. This becomes your mind focusing point; the key is to remain focused. If you are at a standstill position in your life remember it is temporal, nothing last forever not even the earth despite what you may believe everything that is living must soon parish. Understand the difference between what reality is and what not reality is. What you see is not real; it is only real because you believe it is real. What I mean by this, is you only understand what you understand, you only see what you see. Meaning,

155

what your see as in your thoughts is your reality. Thoughts are only thoughts until you react, but what triggers your thoughts to react? Acceptance, respect, misunderstood, not valued, are not in control, will cause your thoughts to react in an unpleasant manner. Understand your thoughts and control them to the best of your ability. Some people may not agree with me, but sometimes I do not agree with myself I am just being honest. Remember a lie you have to remember the truth you do not. This is very vital in any relationship that you encounter. Men have been said, to have a simple mind, but how is this true when both male and female have the same ability to produce the same results. Each man has his own way of life as well as women. Everyone world is different, no one views life the same. When you find a

156

potential mate, discover their world, and see if it aligns with yours. If not do not proceed, and do not send mixed emotional signals. If you proceed to send mix signals, this will become very dangerous. Human beings are emotional creatures and anything can trigger unfound and unhealed emotions. You may watch the news television and discover many deaths, and suicides based on emotional pain. Having a broken heart may become very dangerous, because the person, whom the broken heart belongs to, is experiencing a feeling that is not curable instantly. A person suffering from this emotional turbulence may have no limits, and sometimes having no limits will produce revenge against the person who has caused there broken heart. This emotion is only curable by time. This is when time is at its best, days become nights and nights become days. Some may mistake this as love, but love does not cause pain, pain causes pain. If you ever were, hurt by anyone, and it does not matter who has hurt you, forgive him or her. You are forgiving them, because this is the only way to heal your recently open wound. It is sad, but some people live with a broken heart for the remainder of their life. A brokenhearted spirit will gravitate, other brokenhearted spirits. This is how it continues to live from one person to another. Break this cycle, force yourself to learn yourself through emotional turbulence, and realize that this will lead to a victory triumph. A wise woman by the name of Maya Angelou once said," You may encounter many defeats, but you must not be defeated. In fact it may be necessary to encounter the defeats, so you can know who you are, what you can rise from, how you can still come out of it'. Every situation you face in life is supposed to happen it was already predestined. This situations, is what shapes your life. Never let it change your life but assist in making your life better. Begin to work with your current mate, open your heart and expose your wounds, so your companion will force theirs as well. Accomplishing, this will produce a bond that will always last and never parish, even if you two decide to separate. When a person find a person whom they can confide in, it causes the heart to open more deeply and speak words that have never been, spoken it is very vital to find this type of person, for your own self and personal self-worth. Remember that the only thing that exists at this moment is what you are doing now. Nothing

else matters until it matters.

Chapter 9

Open your mind and understand who you are. No one is you there is only, one you. You are unique in your own individual way! Never let anyone say, differently. Appreciate who you are and value your life, stand up to what you believe in. If you love your mate then share it with the world. Never hesitate! There will be many in your life that will try to alter you decisions; these are people, you should avoid, because they are in a world that only exists to them. Have you heard, the saying, Mom is all ways right? Well, to be honest this is not true. It may seem true, because we value and respect our mothers sayings (at least some do) but they are human a make mistakes as well. Some mothers want the best for their child, and there may be a select few, that is opposite.

161

All advice is just what it sounds like advice. It is up to you to accept it or reject it. Pay attention to everyone you met, watch signs and body language at all time. Therefore, listen to whom you decide has vital information that you can implement into your life. Take what you can use from the conversation and disregard the rest. When you are interacting with someone new, it is always important information available if you discover your purpose for meeting him or her. This is something to think about, nothing is randomly, there is nothing existing that is not supposed to exist. Make no assumptions question everything. Your companion depends on you weather you believe it, or not. Most men look for women that are similar to the woman in his life, with that being said; understand that the woman in your mate's life has a very important role in your companion's life. It is very wrong to become jealous of these types of relationships; it will only produce negative presumptions about the woman whom he chooses to engaged. Once the women of your mate's family perceives, negative images and thoughts, this leads the man into resentfulness towards his mate. When a man faces this situation, it forces him to make an unfair decision. He has to choose between his family and his companion, choosing his family first will devastate the woman, whom he confides in the most. Choosing his mate over his family will leave his family feeling hurt as well. You see sometimes the people in our family; do not want to let you go. They pretend but there actions say otherwise. This may be a bond, which you do not know exist. Most human beings tend to react when forced to react. Therefore, you will not understand the bond until you recognize the bond. I have seen many mothers choosing are having a say so on who their daughters or son should date or marry, this is wrong. Because we are all unique individuals, we look, smell, hear and speak differently. So what your parents may think is only their opinion it is up to you to accept it or not. Either accept it or reject it but I encourage you to choose wisely. Now please do not interpret the actual message that I am trying to get across, I am not saying do not listen to your parents, not at all. What I am saying is be mindful to the information you receive and whom you receive it from. Do not take advice from a person who does not implement his or her own advice. A woman that has been married numerous times and is now divorced probably would not be the best person to receive marriage advice. You would not ask a mechanic, how to fix a broken leg, and you would not ask a doctor how to change oil. Think about it! So why would you ask a person a question when they have no knowledge in the field you are asking in? Therefore, ask a person about marriage advice that has been married once and is currently still married. The problem with many individuals is that they seem to believe anything and not question if it is a fact or opinion. Facts, proven statements; opinions are individuals thoughts and ideas. What are your proven facts of yourself, do you know your actual birthday? Alternatively, do you know someone else's opinion is it a fact that you were born on that particular day? No, it is not. You were born thousands of years ago; in dreams sometimes, you witness the past events that have occurred in your pervious life, similar to de javu. There is a time and date, which must be documented; this is to keep order of your life from birth to death a record of your existence. However, in reality it does not exist. Time is just an illusion it is only to enhance structure and order. I society eliminates time, what would the world become. If you eliminate the man what would the world become, as well as eliminating the woman, what would happen these are questions that people are afraid to ask as well as know the correct answer. When you think of questions of this nature, it forces the mind to utilize it conscious mind, if you think and ponder on anything for a long time it will eventually manifest. It does not matter, what the thought maybe, and good or bad, it will prosper. Now let us look at the positive side. Think about a great everlasting fruitful relationship picture the way you want you companion to be, in your mind. If you continue to ponder on this thought, it will begin to grow into a reality. The key is when it happens recognize that it is happening and embrace it. Some humans ask the universe things and when they receive what they want they question what they ask for, how ironic is this! Think and receive! This will only happen when you understand what you are thinking. If you desire to become great, and then plant greatness in your mind, water it with thoughts and watch it grow. Whatever you decide to plant in your mind, realize that it will become your reality, no one else only yours. Be careful not to mistake reality with lies. Reality is what you see, hear and feel. Lies are the complete opposite. Do not confuse your mind it is, complex enough. Adding thoughts that are more complex will disable your mind future advancements. Understand whom you are and if you are unsure, of whom you are ask yourself. Where you are now in life, relationships, career, this will help you determine who you are, The question is are you happy with yourself at this point in life if you answer yes great, if you answer no, then you must relearn yourself in order to understand yourself. Where you are currently in your life relates to the decisions and choices you chose. Where you live, who your committed too, where you work the type of vehicle you drive is based on choices that you as an individual have made. If you want to receive, the best things in life then make the best decisions. Many people fail themselves, and sometimes we as human beings shatter our own dreams. We seem to blame others for our choices and decisions, when solely we are the one to blame. Look over your life, what have you accomplished. Is your life worthy, perhaps worthy enough for someone to write a book based on your life? Think about it. Choices are the key, when you make any choice you must put full thought into the choices you make. The only way to make the best decisions in life is by understanding why you are making a choice in the first place. This is why it is extremely important to choose the right companion; this is very vital and critical. The mate you choose will have a major effect on your life, once you enter their world. Now their world may be totally opposite from your world, but this is when you implement your thoughts and desires into their unfamiliar world. By doing this you will begin to discover a different outlook on the human mind. A mind that is easy accessible, understand that knowledge is power, but knowledge of your own mind is greater. Therefore help increase the knowledge of your future companion mind, and they will thank you forever. There may be danger when implementing this, I say this because, your future mate may think you are playing mental games and humans do not like anyone to play mental or emotional games. Therefore, this is very important to stress to your future companion that you are not doing such a thing. Express that you are trying to tap into their core existence to

find and understand whom they really are.

Chapter 10

Only understand you! You are what matters the most to you. Be very selective on who you choose to invite in your life weather is friends or future companions. Never put all your trust into another human being not even your current spouse or companion will always disappoint you. Make no assumptions, but only trust you. If you decide to trust, anyone place limitations on your trust barrier. If not, pain will become your destiny, for pain and hurt that will last a lifetime. Some individuals heal quickly while others live inside their pain, what I mean by live inside their pain is living inside their wounds that have not had the proper time to heal .Some forgive and forget while others forget and not forgive. If your mate is a great person inside in and out then show love and gratitude towards them. Never give up on them because with you, the may discover their true existence. First, it starts with you and only you. You will hear negative opinion's about whom you choose to be with, but understand that's all it is, is opinions and they do not matter unless you make them matter. Once you merge life with someone then life becomes a new world, but only to the eyes that recognize the change.

You cannot change anyone, but you can assist him or her in his or her journey of change. Women build your man up, encourage him and do not make him feel less than a man, I have noticed that many women do not encourage their man, but some do. The women that do encourage their mate are happy, because in order to encourage someone you must first learn how to encourage yourself. Therefore, the woman that has conquered this is happy and life is a great breeze. The women that have trouble in this area must learn how to encourage themselves first. For an example, you must learn how to live alone before you are able to live with another human being, because when you live with someone, you begin to merge uncommon ways and destructive patterns, this goes into the old saying, in order to know someone you must first learn to live with them. If overlooked then you may miss a few critical points in discovering who a person truly is. Only believe in what you cannot see and not what you see. A person may become eye candy but beneath the inner shell their rotten like the core of an apple. This is why I explained, the importance of understanding a person mind and true intentions first before you decide to further any relationship that you think may be an everlasting one always dig to understand there ulterior motives if there is one at all. This goes back to understanding, the choices you make, and you must dissect every choice. Proper preparation prevents poor performance. Change the way you think and overcome each obstacle that you may come against. Now there will be tension

Volume 1

especially when you become a distant being to others but realize you cannot pay that any mind. Many successful people have learned how to distant themselves in order to accomplish their greatness. Some distant themselves to save them from further hurt, understand running away from a problem only enhances the problem. So face the problem at hand because history repeats itself and you will face the exact problem once again. No matter if its relationship wise, or in life general, it will resurface. What you do when it resurface is totally up to you! Prepare yourself for unseen battles they will come through many unseen avenues. Properly prepare yourself mentally, spiritually and physically. Sometimes you may need, to rely on the universe to guide you, and trust me it will always direct you in the way you should go. Do not interpret this the wrong way, but the universe as well as the higher power is the key to conquering anything that this world has to offer. Now departing this world has other requirements as well. In addition, yes there are requirements that are required before leaving this earth. There are roads that a person must take before leaving this earth. Once a person leave this earth whatever they were supposed to accomplish they have already accomplished, you may not know what their destiny may have been, but there destiny was accomplished otherwise they would have not departed. Many do not know there destiny and others do, once you realize your destiny then your life is accomplished, whether young or old. In other to achieve your destiny you must find your other half the part that completes

Volume 1

you, many may say a significant other but I say the side of you that you have not discovered. You complete you! Another human being cannot add to your completeness but limit your completeness. Another human being may assist you and help you strive to become completed but you must complete yourself first there is no other way to explain it. A man was born alone and a woman was born alone as well. Therefore, you must do everything on your own accordance. Pay attention to your own flaws and disappointments and you will be able to recognize others frequently. Only once you understand your mistakes, you will be able to benefit from others. Conquer anything that opposes you, a challenge is the door, which will guarantee your success. Do not give up on anything, which you choose to challenge this will only, make you greater this is a promise from me to you. You are important if not to anyone in this world, you are important to yourself. Do not give up on yourself sometimes we can become our own worst enemy without even realizing it. We hurt ourselves more than we allow others to. We are destruction to ourselves. This must become obsolete, when this begins to occur then life will become a world that we share with others that have followed these concepts.

TO BE CONTNUED……

Volume 1